Terrific
TABBIES

SPOTTED! STRIPED!

CLASSIC! TICKED!

ABDO
Publishing Company

Katherine Hengel

Consulting Editor, Diane Craig, M.A./Reading Specialist

visit us at www.abdopublishing.com

Published by ABDO Publishing Company, a division of ABDO, P.O. Box 398166, Minneapolis, Minnesota 55439. Copyright © 2012 by Abdo Consulting Group, Inc. International copyrights reserved in all countries. No part of this book may be reproduced in any form without written permission from the publisher. Super SandCastle™ is a trademark and logo of ABDO Publishing Company.

Printed in the United States of America, North Mankato, Minnesota
062011
092011

♻ PRINTED ON RECYCLED PAPER

Editor: Liz Salzmann
Content Developer: Nancy Tuminelly
Cover and Interior Design and Production:
 Anders Hanson, Mighty Media
Illustrations: Bob Doucet
Photo Credits: Shutterstock

Library of Congress Cataloging-in-Publication Data
Hengel, Katherine.
 Terrific tabbies / authored by Katherine Hengel ; illustrated by Bob Doucet.
   p. cm. -- (Cat craze set 2)
 ISBN 978-1-61714-834-7
 1. Tabby cats--Juvenile literature. I. Doucet, Bob, ill. II. Title.
 SF449.T32H46 2012
 636.8--dc22
                        2010053266

Super SandCastle™ books are created by a team of professional educators, reading specialists, and content developers around five essential components—phonemic awareness, phonics, vocabulary, text comprehension, and fluency—to assist young readers as they develop reading skills and strategies and increase their general knowledge. All books are written, reviewed, and leveled for guided reading, early reading intervention, and Accelerated Reader® programs for use in shared, guided, and independent reading and writing activities to support a balanced approach to literacy instruction.

CONTENTS

The Tabby	3
Coat Types	4
Health & Care	8
Attitude & Behavior	10
Litters & Kittens	12
Buying a Tabby	14
Living with a Tabby	18
What's in a Name?	20
Find the Tabby	22
The Tabby Quiz	23
Glossary	24

The
TABBY

Tabby is not a cat **breed**. It is a type of coat. Many breeds of cats have tabby coats. Tabbies have special markings. They may have stripes, spots, or other patterns. Most tabby cats have an M-shaped mark on their heads. Their chins are **usually** white.

COAT TYPES

There are four main types of tabby coats. They are mackerel, spotted, classic, and ticked. Tabbies may have any color of fur.

Mackerel Tabby

Most tabbies are mackerel tabbies. Thin stripes of dark fur cover most of their coats.

Like most tabbies, they have an M-shaped mark on their heads. Their chins are white. They have lines that go from their eyes down their cheeks. These are called "**bandit**" or "glasses" lines.

MACKEREL TABBY

Spotted Tabby

A spotted tabby has stripes on its face, legs, and tail. Its sides have spots instead of stripes. The spots may be large or small.

SPOTTED TABBY

Classic Tabby

Classic tabbies are also called **blotched** tabbies. They have wide stripes and blotches of dark fur. These shapes are often **swirly**. They may look like they have bull's-eyes on their sides.

CLASSIC TABBY

Ticked Tabby

Ticked tabbies don't have clear patterns. Their light and dark hairs are spread around more evenly. This gives their coats a salt-and-pepper look. Ticked tabbies may have stripes on their faces, legs, stomachs, and tails.

TICKED TABBY

HEALTH & CARE

Life Span

Tabby cats can live for 15 years or longer!

Health Concerns

Tabby cats do not have any special health **concerns**.

8

VET'S CHECKLIST

- Have your tabby spayed or neutered. This will prevent unwanted kittens.

- Visit a vet for regular checkups.

- Clean your tabby cat's teeth and ears once a week.

- Ask your vet about shots that may benefit your cat.

- Ask your vet which foods are right for your tabby.

ATTITUDE & BEHAVIOR

Personality

Like most cats, tabbies are curious and independent. They like being petted and cuddled. They also like to be left alone sometimes. They often bond with the person who feeds them.

Activity Level

Tabbies are very active when they are less than one year old. As a cat gets older, it spends more time resting.

All About Me

Hi! My name is Tommy. I'm a tabby. I just wanted to let you know a few things about me. I made some lists below of things I like and dislike. Check them out!

Things I Like

- Jumping and climbing to high places
- Being petted by my owner
- Eating meaty treats
- Playing with toys
- Following my owner around the house
- Getting a lot of attention

Things I Dislike

- Other cats that I don't know
- Getting dirty or wet
- Being bored

LITTERS & KITTENS

Litter Size

Female tabbies give birth to two to ten kittens.

Diet

Newborn kittens drink their mother's milk. They can begin to eat kitten food when they are about six weeks old. Kitten food is different from cat food. It has the extra **protein**, fat, **vitamins**, and **minerals** that kittens need to grow.

Growth

Tabby kittens should stay with their mothers until they are three months old. A kitten will be almost full grown when it is six months old. But it will continue to grow slowly until it is one year old.

BUYING A TABBY

Choosing a Breeder

It's best to buy a kitten from a **breeder**, not a pet store. When you visit a cat breeder, ask to see the mother and father of the kittens. Make sure the parents are healthy, friendly, and well behaved.

Picking a Kitten

Choose a kitten that isn't too active or too shy. If you sit down, some of the kittens may come over to you. One of them might be the right one for you!

14

Is It the Right Pet for You?

Buying a cat is a big decision. You'll want to make sure your new pet suits your lifestyle.

Get out a piece of paper. Draw a line down the middle.

Read the statements listed here. Each time you agree with a statement from the left column, make a mark on the left side of your paper. When you agree with a statement from the right column, make a mark on the right side of your paper.

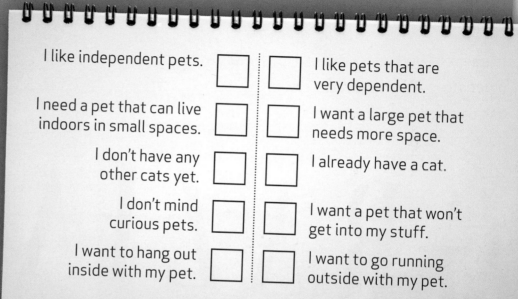

I like independent pets.	☐	☐	I like pets that are very dependent.
I need a pet that can live indoors in small spaces.	☐	☐	I want a large pet that needs more space.
I don't have any other cats yet.	☐	☐	I already have a cat.
I don't mind curious pets.	☐	☐	I want a pet that won't get into my stuff.
I want to hang out inside with my pet.	☐	☐	I want to go running outside with my pet.

If you made more marks on the left side than on the right side, a cat may be the right pet for you! If you made more marks on the right side of your paper, you might want to consider another pet.

Some Things You'll Need

Cats go to the bathroom in a **litter box**. It should be kept in a quiet place. Most cats learn to use their litter box all by themselves. You just have to show them where it is! The dirty **litter** should be scooped out every day. The litter should be changed completely every week.

Your cat's **food and water dishes** should be wide and shallow. This helps your cat keep its whiskers clean. The dishes should be in a different area than the litter box. Cats do not like to eat and go to the bathroom in the same area.

Cats love to scratch! **Scratching posts** help keep cats from scratching the furniture. The scratching post should be taller than your cat. It should have a wide, heavy base so it won't tip over.

Cats are natural predators. Without small animals to hunt, cats may become bored and unhappy. **Cat toys** can satisfy your cat's need to chase and capture. They will help keep your cat entertained and happy.

Cats should not play with balls of yarn or string. If they accidentally eat the yarn, they could get sick.

Cat claws should be trimmed regularly with special cat claw **clippers**. Regular nail clippers will also work. Some people choose to have their cat's claws removed by a vet. But most vets and animal rights groups think declawing is cruel.

You should brush your cat regularly with a **cat hair brush**. This will help keep its coat healthy and clean.

A **cat bed** will give your cat a safe, comfortable place to sleep.

LIVING WITH A TABBY

Being a Good Companion

Tabby cats are social animals. They love to be close to their owners. So, let your tabby know that you love it every day!

Pet your tabby often. Good spots are behind the ears, under the chin, and above the tail. If your cat rolls over, softly pet its tummy!

Inside or Outside?

Most vets and **breeders** agree that it is best for cats to be kept inside. That way the cats are safe from predators and cars.

Feeding Your Tabby

Tabbies may be fed regular cat food. Your vet can help you choose the best food for your cat.

Cleaning the Litter Box

Like all cats, tabbies like to be clean. They don't like smelly or dirty litter boxes. If the litter box is dirty, they may go to the bathroom somewhere else. Ask your vet for advice if your cat isn't using its box.

 **DANGER: POISONOUS FOODS**

Some people like to feed their cats table scraps. Here are some human foods that can make cats sick.

TOMATOES

POTATOES

ONIONS

GARLIC

CHOCOLATE

GRAPES

WHAT'S IN A NAME?

The word *tabby* comes from the French word *tabis*. *Tabis* was the French name for a type of **silk** made in Iraq. The silk was striped, just like mackerel tabby cats.

French people brought the **silk** back from Iraq. Then they brought it to England. English people saw that the *tabis* looked like the fur of some cats. They began to call such cats *tabbies*!

FIND THE TABBY

A

B

C

D

THE TABBY QUIZ

1. Tabby is a **breed** of cat. **True or false?**

2. Mackerel tabbies have thin stripes. **True or false?**

3. Mackerel tabbies are spotted. **True or false?**

4. Young tabby cats are active. **True or false?**

5. Tabbies like to be far away from their owners. **True or false?**

6. The word *tabby* comes from a French word. **True or false?**

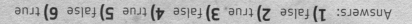

Answers: 1) false 2) true 3) false 4) true 5) false 6) true

GLOSSARY

bandit - a robber or outlaw, especially one who wears a mask.

blotch - an uneven spot of color.

breed - a group of animals or plants with common ancestors. A *breeder* is someone whose job is to breed certain animals or plants.

concern - a problem or worry.

mineral - a natural element that plants, animals, and people need to be healthy.

protein - a substance found in all plant and animal cells.

silk - a kind of cloth that is very soft and smooth.

swirly - having a rounded or spiral pattern or shape.

usually - commonly or normally.

vitamin - a substance needed for good health, found naturally in plants and meats.